1⁰⁰

Bouquet
of
Memories
for
Mother

Published in the United States by Mark Publishing, 1988
ISBN 0-937769-06-1

Copyright © 1988

Produced by
Mark Publishing
15 Camp Evers Ln.
Scotts Valley, CA 95066

Poetry: **Frank Carpenter**
Photography: **Rick Browne**
Illustrations: **Mary Ann Riemer**
Editor: **Judi Williams**
Printed in Hong Kong

About the Author

Frank Carpenter's literary talents were first discovered adorning the walls of the Carpenter family ranch in Eastern Oklahoma during a visit by our editor. This young poet, who is a devoted husband and father of two small children, now makes his home in Southern California.

In this first published collection, Frank captures the warmth and tenderness of the memorable moments in our lives.

Especially for Mothers and Grandmothers, life is very much like a bouquet of flowers. Each memory of those you love is a flower in the bouquet of your life. May the pages of this book enhance the beauty and fragrance of your bouquet.

When I hold
my precious baby,
I'm filled with joy
and wonder. . .

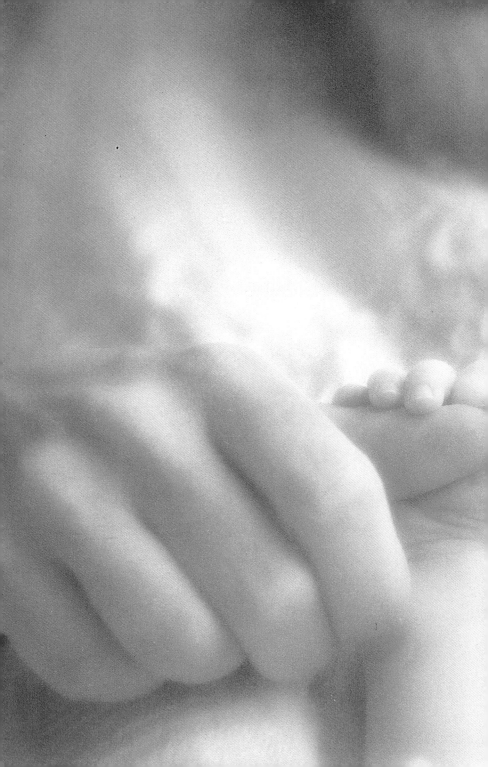

Five Small Fingers

*When five small fingers
grasp one big thumb,
the cares of the world
are overcome.*

Cherished Times

As much as I long
for quiet times
when the children are fast asleep,
the memories of them
when they're awake
are the ones I will cherish and keep.

My Baby Girl

My beautiful baby girl
playing outside on the lawn
without a care in the world. . .
but soon you will be gone.

When you were born I couldn't believe
how much you looked like me,
an image so clear none could deny
and all could plainly see.

My little one won't stay at home
forever in the yard,
a time will come when I'll let go
and I know it will be hard.

I'm sure the happiness I've known
will stay here in my heart
long after you are fully grown,
and we are far apart.

But no matter where you go
in this wide and wondrous world,
I'll always treasure you, my dear,
as my special baby girl.

These Precious Years

Lord,
let me not be so burdened
with caring for my children
that I forget about
enjoying my children.

While cleaning
up the mess
they made,
help me to remember
how much fun they
had in making it.

Help me to make the most
of these precious years
when my children are mine
to train,
and to love.

The Rocking Chair

*I couldn't count
the sleepless nights
I spent in that rocking chair,
but I'd never trade
those precious times
with my baby there.*

Naptime

I came home early
from the office today
and the sight that greeted me,
was my wife with our baby
asleep in her arms
in sweet serenity.
I wanted to wake them
and whisper hello
but I knew it was for the best
to give them this moment together
and quietly let them rest.

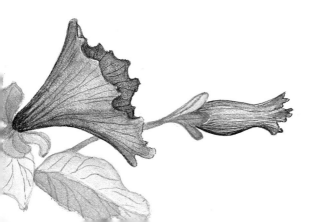

For you, my child,
everything is new and exciting
and I love being here
to share it with you . . .

All the Thanks That I Need

You wake up too early each morning.
You soil your brand new shirt.
You won't eat a decent breakfast,
then you swallow a handful of dirt.
But just when I'm reaching my limit
a hoarse little voice says to me,
"Mommy, I love you the mostest!"
and that's all the thanks that I need.

Little Things

Cracker crumbs
on the kitchen floor,
crayon pictures
on the ice box door.
Popsicle sticks
and baseball cards,
balls and tricycles
in the yard.

These things that could drive
some people mad
are welcome sights
that make me glad.

My Hand in Yours

Whenever something frightens me
and makes me feel so small. . .
I simply put my hand in yours
and all at once
I'm tall.

Her Vision

Watching and waiting,
anticipating
the adults they'll someday be.
While others stand by
only hearing them cry,
lacking the vision to see.

But undaunted and proud
of her small, precious crowd,
mother takes care of their needs.
Seeing God's wisdom,
and knowing His kingdom,
begins with such babes as these.

My Miracle

I thank God most every day
for what you are, my dear.
I must believe in miracles
when I see you standing here.
And more important, dearest child,
I know that God is real.
For only He could be the source
of all the love I feel.

Muddy Sneakers

A pair of muddy sneakers
left lying by the door,
tell the tale of a daring journey
or an ancient medieval war.
Perhaps a brave explorer
crossed the river to Timbuktu,
or was forced to hide in a swamp
while a band of Apaches rode through.
Perhaps the top law man in Texas
had to stand ankle-deep in wet sand,
while he watered his gleaming stallion
on the bank of the Rio Grande...

More likely my brave little hero
played in sprinklers along the way
but he'd never admit that to mother...
And I'd have it no other way.

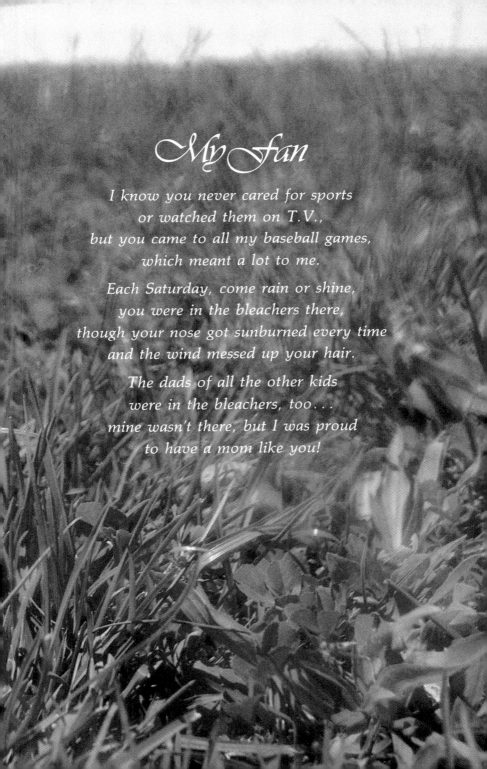

My Fan

I know you never cared for sports
or watched them on T.V.,
but you came to all my baseball games,
which meant a lot to me.

Each Saturday, come rain or shine,
you were in the bleachers there,
though your nose got sunburned every time
and the wind messed up your hair.

The dads of all the other kids
were in the bleachers, too...
mine wasn't there, but I was proud
to have a mom like you!

My Playmate

The other moms
I see at the park
are busy with gossip and books,
occasionally giving
reprimands,
glances or sidelong looks.
But my mom
always swings with me
and waits at the end of the slide.
On the merry-go-round
or the jungle gym,
she's right there by my side.

Through Your Eyes

I see within your eyes
forgotten seasons of my life,
when the sky was bluer
the grass was greener
and I was more alive.

Back then my dreams were
more than dreams
they were much larger
so it seemed

now through your young
and wondering eyes
I can see anew,
the world seems bigger
the sun shines brighter
for I feel young
through you.

You aren't a child anymore,
your teenage years are here.
We still have so much to learn…

Spreading Wings

You don't understand what
I'm talking about
That's it, I quit, I'm moving out!
Do what you think you have to do
but your father and I will still love you.

I can't be the person you want me to be
I have to escape, I need to be free!
We support you no matter what you do,
and I understand what you're going through.

I'm sorry for all the things that I said
being eighteen sort of went to my head.
Sometimes I forget that you're still my mom . . .
by the way, can I use the car for the prom?

Values

I never liked or understood
so many things you did.
You made my life so difficult,
and you treated me like a kid.

It seemed throughout my teen-age years
we disagreed a lot.
In fact, I guess that you could say
we often truly fought.

But now I see that I was wrong,
and all you ever did
was try to teach your values
to a strong-willed, stubborn kid.

My Friend

Your Adolescence
has come to an end,
no longer my baby
now you're my friend.

Tough Love

Yes, you have to clean your room.
No, you may not stay out late.
And you can't wear faded jeans
when going on a date.
You're far too young to drive our car.
Now don't you talk that way. . .
as long as you live in this house,
I'll have the final say.

You may not understand,
it takes a love that's tough
to bring out the inner beauty
of a diamond in the rough.

The Parting Gift

I'm not moved out, but I'm almost packed,
so I'm practicing writing home.
Even though I haven't left,
I'm starting to feel alone.

I've grown so used to having you
around to help me out...
whenever a problem came my way
you helped me through my doubt.

And now, as I stand here at the brink
of starting a new life,
I'll always cherish your example
as a mother and a wife.

Thank you, Mom, for all you've done.
Now I clearly see,
the memories that we have shared
are your parting gift to me.

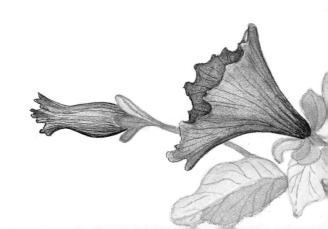

Daughter of Mine

*I've done the best
that I know how. . .
It's up to you,
and the time is now.
I've given you all
a mother could give,
but you have your own
special life to live.
You are almost a woman,
O daughter of mine,
and I want you to know
that you're doing just fine.*

*I enjoyed
all those years
of raising you,
but now that you're an adult
it's nice to have you
as my friend. . .*

A Mother's Victory

Blessed are the children
of a woman who loves them.
Proud is the mother
who raises them well...
And when they're grown,
their success is her victory...
For she taught them how
to believe in themselves.

Patches

I know it's been a while
since I wrote you last.
I've been too busy to notice
how quickly the weeks have passed.
But last weekend while the kids
were skiing with some friends,
we began to clean the attic. . .
getting rid of some odds and ends.

We came across a tattered box
at the bottom of a pile
of dusty things we hadn't seen
or used for quite a while.
What was in that ragged box?
My old blanket, frayed and torn,
and a pair of small, patched jeans
that I had often worn.

I must have been just five or six
when I wore those faded jeans. . .
but no one knew except for me
how much those pants could mean.
Why did I save those ragged jeans
for years up in the box?
I didn't save my shirts or coats,
my shoes or hats or socks.

What made them special though, you see
was not the rips or tears
but the loving way you faithfully
made the many repairs.

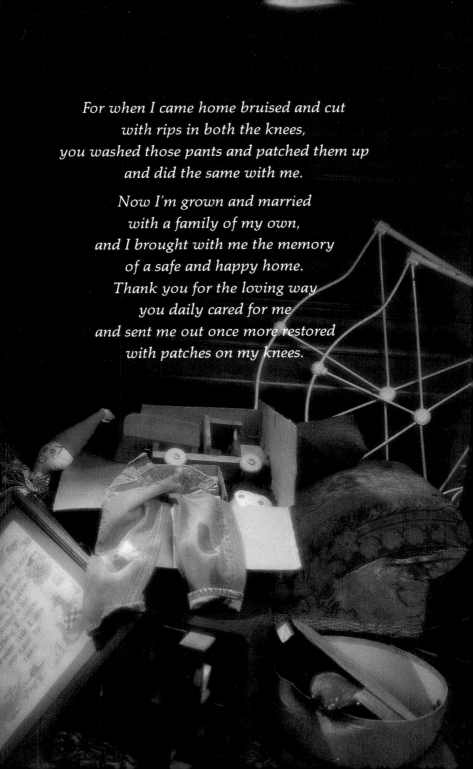

For when I came home bruised and cut
with rips in both the knees,
you washed those pants and patched them up
and did the same with me.

Now I'm grown and married
with a family of my own,
and I brought with me the memory
of a safe and happy home.
Thank you for the loving way
you daily cared for me
and sent me out once more restored
with patches on my knees.

Thank You Mom

You were the first to hold me . . .
you comforted me through many nights.
You fed me,
you dressed me,
you taught me to walk.
Sometimes you scolded me,
but you never stopped loving me.
Now I am older,
I have a daughter of my own,
and I finally understand
what you did for me.
Now it is time to say, "Thank You, Mom!"

The Swingset

A rusty swingset stands solemnly
in the back yard. . .
a monument to days long gone
when children laughed and played,
of summer days spent on the lawn
and many memories made.

Best of Friends

*The best of friends
don't meet by chance
or the result of circumstance.
The best of friends
you will ever see
are mothers and daughters...
like you and me.*

Now that I'm a grandmother,
I'm taking
all the time I want
to enjoy the children in my life...

Storytime

Almost anyone can read,
but when you read to me
you bring alive a magic world
that I can clearly see.
As I sit upon your lap
and watch the pages turn,
I'm lost on voyages far away…
I listen and I learn.
You never ever skip a page
like others often do.
You know that my excitement
comes from deep inside of you.
You always change your voice a bit
when villains are about,
and when you feel the time is right
you're not afraid to shout!
But the thing that means the most to me
after a book is done,
is when I hear you say…
"Let's read another one!"

One More

Grandma, I love you.
You always have the
time for. . .
one more game
one more book
one more hug
one more song
one more program
one more anything.
You make me feel important!

The Things You Do

I like to go on walks with you
'cause you walk slow like me.
Most adults take such big steps,
they're always in a hurry.

I like it when you sing to me,
and when I sing for you.
I teach you songs I learn at school,
and you teach me songs, too.

I like it when you tell me jokes
or tickle me awhile,
because that makes me laugh out loud,
and also makes you smile.

But Grandma, what I like the most
about the things you do...
is how they show your love for me
and that makes me love you.

Holding My Baby

Holding my baby
watching her walk
growing so quickly
learning to talk.
First day at school
a gown for the prom
college, a husband,
and then she's a mom.

Holding my granddaughter
watching her walk
growing so quickly
learning to talk.
Where did the years go?
I must make the time,
for holding this baby
granddaughter of mine.

Legacy of Love

*You taught my mother to be
a mom
and now she's teaching me.
Someday I'll have
a daughter,
and she'll be your
legacy.*

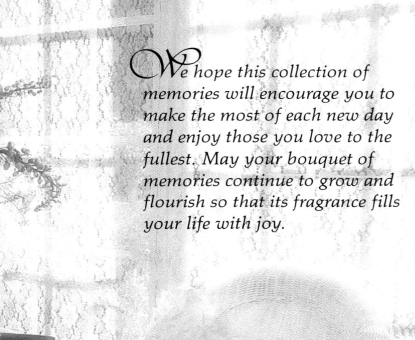

We hope this collection of memories will encourage you to make the most of each new day and enjoy those you love to the fullest. May your bouquet of memories continue to grow and flourish so that its fragrance fills your life with joy.